MEASURING AND COMPARING

How Long is Long?
Comparing Animals

Vic Parker

Raintree

www.raintreepublishers.co.uk
Visit our website to find out more information about Raintree books.

To order:
☎ Phone 0845 6044371
🖷 Fax +44 (0) 1865 312263
🖳 Email myorders@raintreepublishers.co.uk

Customers from outside the UK please telephone +44 1865 312262

Raintree is an imprint of Capstone Global Library Limited, a company incorporated in England and Wales having its registered office at 7 Pilgrim Street, London, EC4V 6LB – Registered company number: 6695582

Text © Capstone Global Library Limited 2011
First published in hardback in 2011
The moral rights of the proprietor have been asserted.

Edited by Nancy Dickmann, Rebecca Rissman, and Sian Smith
Designed by Victoria Allen
Picture research by Hannah Taylor
Original illustrations © Capstone Global Library Ltd
Original illustrations by Victoria Allen
Production by Victoria Fitzgerald
Originated by Dot Gradations Ltd
Printed and bound in China by South China Printing Company Ltd

ISBN 978 0 431 00681 9
14 13 12 11 10
10 9 8 7 6 5 4 3 2 1

British Library Cataloguing in Publication Data
Parker, Victoria.
How long is long? : comparing animals. --
(Measuring and comparing)
1. Length measurement--Juvenile literature. 2. Body size--Juvenile literature.
I. Title II. Series
530.8-dc22

Acknowledgements
The author and publisher are grateful to the following for permission to reproduce copyright material: Alamy Images pp.4 (© vario images GmbH & Co.KG), 7 (© Juniors Bildarchiv), 10 (© Hornbil Images); © Capstone Publishers pp.5, 26, 27 (Karon Dubke); Corbis pp.6 (DLILLC), 18 (Momatiuk); FLPA p.24 (Minden Pictures/ Flip Nicklin); istockphoto pp.8 (© Fusun Genc), 14 (© youding xie); naturepl.com pp.12 (Gabriel Rojo), 16 (Andy Rouse); Photolibrary pp.20 (Dea/ C Dani-I. Jeske), 22 (M Krishnan).

Photographs used to create silhouettes: istockphoto, squirrel (© Laurence Dean); shutterstock, foot (© andrisr), rat (© basel101658), peacock (© Vule), tiger (© gaga), crocodile/ whale (© Svetlana Eltsova).

Cover photograph of a male Ebony Jewelwing damselfly reproduced with permission of Photolibrary (Don Johnston).

Every effort has been made to contact copyright holders of material reproduced in this book. Any omissions will be rectified in subsequent printings if notice is given to the publisher.

Disclaimer
All the Internet addresses (URLs) given in this book were valid at the time of going to press. However, due to the dynamic nature of the Internet, some addresses may have changed or ceased to exist since publication. While the author and publisher regret any inconvenience this may cause readers, no responsibility for any such changes can be accepted by either the author or the publisher.

Contents

Words appearing in the text in bold, **like this**,
are explained in the glossary.

What is length?

The length of something is how long it is from end to end. Some things, such as railway tracks, are long. Other things, such as trains, are shorter.

Trains are made up of carriages. Longer trains have more carriages.

To measure length you can use a ruler or a tape measure. These are marked in millimetres (mm), centimetres (cm), and metres (m).

Using a tape measure is sometimes easier with two people.

Long animals

Some animals are longer than others. Being long helps some animals to move fast. For example, a dolphin has a long body. Water glides over it smoothly. This helps it speed along.

Bottlenose dolphins can be 2 to 4 metres long.

Other animals are long because they have long tails. Long tails can be useful. They can help animals to balance, or to grip things. They can also be used to **communicate**.

A long-tailed macaque's tail is even longer than its body.

How long are your feet?

Have you ever measured how long your feet are? **Compared** to a younger brother or sister's feet, your feet might be very long. But how long is long?

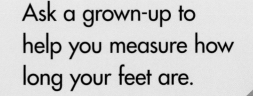

Ask a grown-up to help you measure how long your feet are.

A black rat can be 40 centimetres from the tip of its nose to the end of its tail. A black rat like this would probably be more than twice as long as your foot.

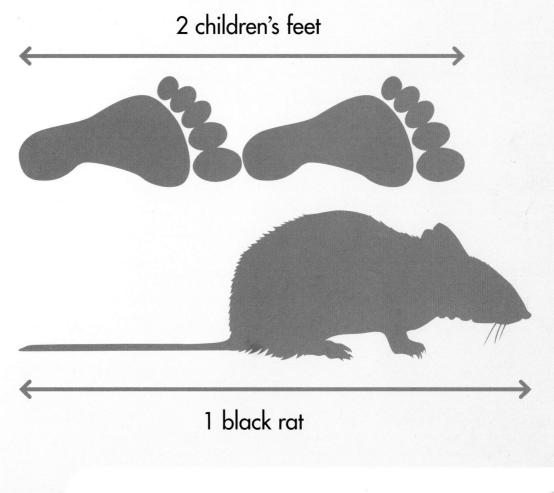

2 children's feet

1 black rat

What is longer than a black rat? ➡

Indian giant squirrel

A squirrel can be longer than a black rat.
The largest type of squirrel is the Indian giant
squirrel. It lives in tall trees in Asia.

Squirrels are **rodents**, like mice and rats.

Indian giant squirrels can grow over 91 centimetres long. If you put two black rats end to end, an Indian giant squirrel would still be longer.

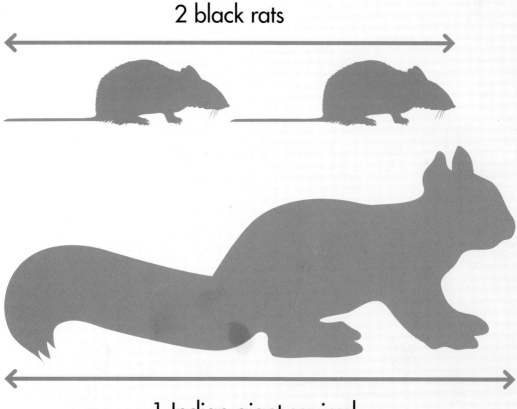

2 black rats

1 Indian giant squirrel

What is longer than a giant squirrel? ➡

Giant armadillo

A giant armadillo is longer than an Indian giant squirrel. Giant armadillos live in forests in South America. They eat **termites** and ants, and sometimes mice and rats.

A giant armadillo has a shell made from overlapping bony scales.

A giant armadillo can measure 1½ metres long. This means that a giant armadillo is more than one and a half times as long as an Indian giant squirrel.

Remember!
100 cm = 1 m

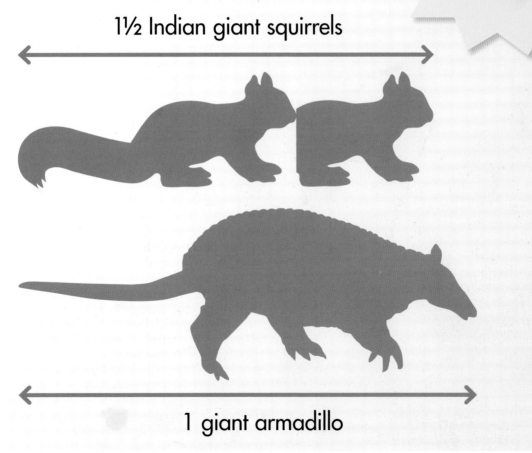

1½ Indian giant squirrels

1 giant armadillo

What is longer than a giant armadillo? ➡️

Peacock

A peacock can be longer than an armadillo. Peacocks have long beautiful tails, called trains. A peacock raises its train to display its stunning feathers.

It can be hard for peacocks to fly when they have such long tails.

A peacock can be just under 3 metres from the tip of its beak to the end of its train. It would take just less than two giant armadillos to be as long as a peacock.

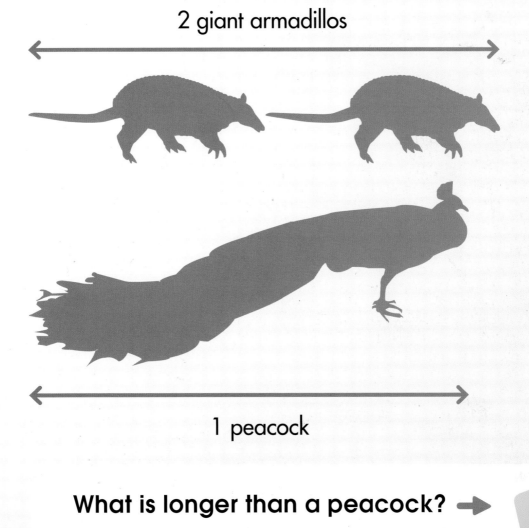

2 giant armadillos

1 peacock

What is longer than a peacock? ➡

Tiger

A tiger is longer than a peacock. Tigers are the longest of all the great cats – even longer than lions. Male tigers are longer than female tigers.

Most tigers have over 100 stripes.

A male tiger can measure up to 4 metres long. This is nearly one and a half times as long as a peacock.

1½ peacocks

1 tiger

What is longer than a tiger? ➡

Southern elephant seal

A Southern elephant seal is longer than a tiger. They are called elephant seals because the males have long noses. They use their noses to make a loud roaring noise.

Male Southern elephant seals are called bulls. Females are called cows.

A bull Southern elephant seal can be 5 metres long. This is one metre longer than a tiger.

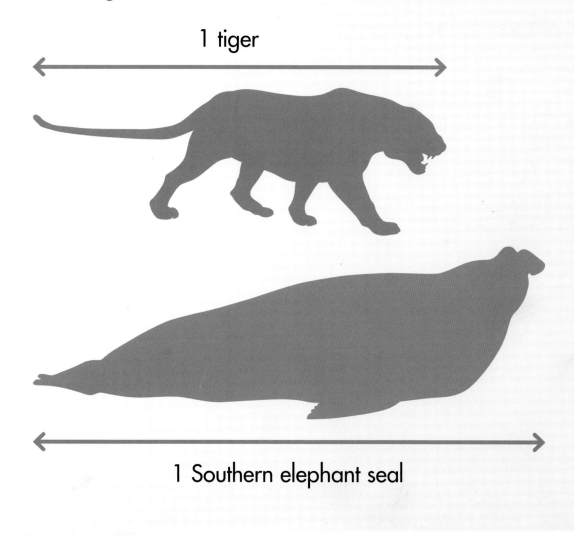

1 tiger

1 Southern elephant seal

What is longer than a seal? ➡

Saltwater crocodile

A saltwater crocodile is longer than a seal. Many saltwater crocodiles live in Northern Australia. They eat animals of all sizes, from small monkeys to huge water buffalo.

Saltwater crocodiles can go for months without catching food.

A male saltwater crocodile can be 6 metres long – sometimes even more. This is longer than a Southern elephant seal and an Indian giant squirrel lined up together.

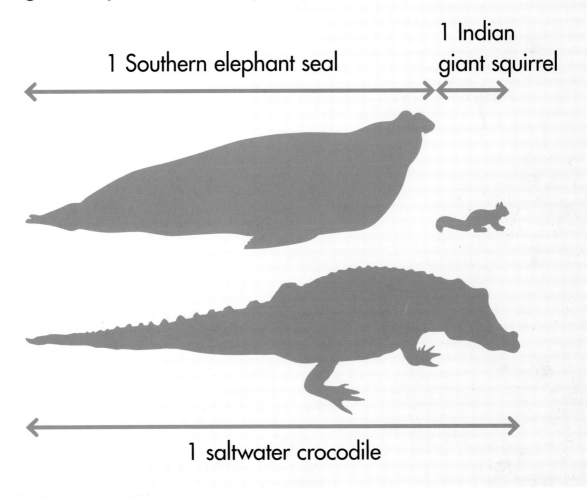

1 Southern elephant seal

1 Indian giant squirrel

1 saltwater crocodile

What is longer than a crocodile? ➡

Python

A python can be longer than a saltwater crocodile. The longest pythons are found in southeast **Asia**. They live in forests and **grasslands** near water. They are good swimmers.

Pythons use their long bodies to wrap around things and grip them tightly.

Pythons are the longest of all snakes. They can be 10 metres long. This is nearly as long as two saltwater crocodiles laid nose to tail.

2 saltwater crocodiles

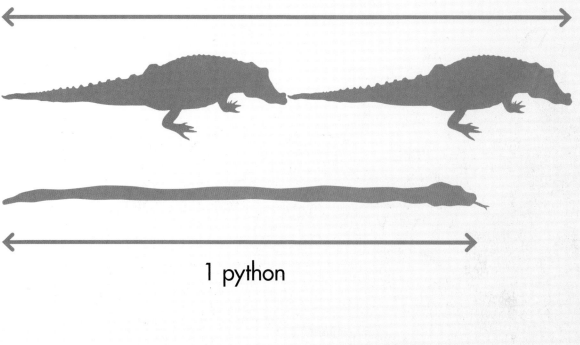

1 python

What is longer than a python? ➡

Blue whale

A blue whale is longer than a python. Blue whales live in the oceans, but they are not fish. They are **mammals**. This means that they feed their babies on milk.

A blue whale breathes when it surfaces, through a blowhole in the top of its head.

Blue whales are bigger than any other animal. They can be over 30 metres long. This is as long as three pythons stretched out end to end, or 75 black rats!

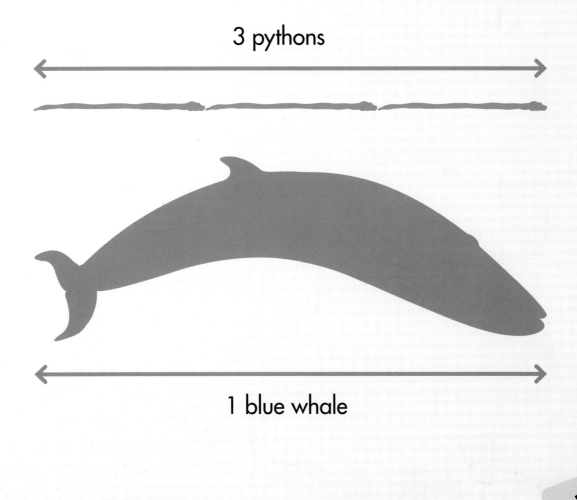

3 pythons

1 blue whale

Measuring activity

Things you will need: a helper, scissors, a tape measure, sticky tape, paper, a pencil, different coloured ribbons, and long objects which you can measure, such as a tennis racket, a scarf, an umbrella, and a table.

1. Work together to cut a piece of ribbon to the same length as your first object.
2. Stretch out the ribbon against the tape measure and measure how long it is in centimetres.

3. Stick the ribbon at the top of a large piece of paper. Write down the name of the object you measured and how long it is in centimetres.

4. Do the same with other long objects, using a different coloured ribbon for each one.

5. Stick the start of each new ribbon right below the last one. This will make it easier to **compare** how long the objects are.

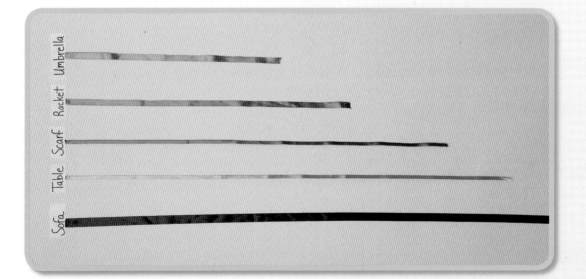

Find out: which object on your chart is the longest?

Long quiz and facts

Small lengths are measured in millimetres (mm).
Larger lengths are measured in centimetres (cm).
Big lengths are measured in metres (m).

Quiz

1. What unit would you use to measure the length of a rabbit?

   a) millimetres   b) centimetres   c) metres

2. What unit would you use to measure the length of an ant?

   a) millimetres   b) centimetres   c) metres

3. What unit would you use to measure the length of a shark?

   a) millimetres   b) centimetres   c) metres

Answers: 1 = b   2 = a   3 = c

Long facts

- A hawk moth's tongue can be up to 30 centimetres long! It uses this long tongue to feed from tall flowers.

- A man called Melvin Boothe has the world's longest fingernails. They measure over 9 metres long!

- The Australian pelican is the bird with the longest beak. Its beak can grow up to 47 centimetres long.

- The world's longest bus is 25 metres long and can hold 300 passengers.

- A giraffe's neck can be about 2 metres long.

- The Amazonian giant centipede can be up to 30 centimetres long. It eats bats, mice, and spiders.

- The longest type of lizard in the world is the Komodo dragon. Many are about 2 to 3 metres long!

Glossary

Asia large part of the world which includes the countries of India, Pakistan, Bangladesh, China, Japan, Indonesia, and Thailand

communicate to give information to someone else. This might be done through making sounds or talking, by writing, or by using parts of the body to make signs.

compare to look at two or more things and see how they are the same and how they are different

grassland area where grass and grass-like plants are the main plants that grow

mammal creature which is warm-blooded and which feeds milk to its young

rodent small furry animal with large teeth. Mice, rats, and rabbits are rodents.

termite insect which eats wood and looks similar to an ant

Find out more

Books

Acorn Plus: Comparing Creatures, Rupert Fandangleman (Raintree Publishers, 2009)

Size and Measurement, Carol Medcalf (Collins, 2008)

Websites

kids.nationalgeographic.com/Animals/
This website is packed with sound clips, videos, and information about different animals.

www.bbc.co.uk/skillswise/e3/numbers/ measuresshapespace/length
Find out about length with the factsheet, quiz, and measuring game on this website.

www.primaryresources.co.uk/maths/mathsE1. htm#length
This website has fun activity sheets on length that you can print and try out.

Index